Pulling Dogs

WORKING
DOGS

By Kristen Rajczak

Gareth Stevens
Publishing

Please visit our Web site, www.garethstevens.com. For a free color catalog of all our high-quality books, call toll free 1-800-542-2595 or fax 1-877-542-2596.

Library of Congress Cataloging-in-Publication Data

Rajczak, Kristen.
Pulling dogs / Kristen Rajczak.
    p. cm. — (Working dogs)
Includes index.
ISBN 978-1-4339-4664-6 (pbk.)
ISBN 978-1-4339-4665-3 (6-pack)
ISBN 978-1-4339-4663-9 (library binding)
1. Sled dogs. I. Title.
SF428.7.R35 2011
636.7'0886—dc22

2010037168

First Edition

Published in 2011 by
Gareth Stevens Publishing
111 East 14th Street, Suite 349
New York, NY 10003

Copyright © 2011 Gareth Stevens Publishing

Designer: Michael J. Flynn
Editor: Kristen Rajczak

Photo credits: Cover, pp. 1, 14 iStockphoto.com; pp. 5, 6, 9, 10, 13, 17, 18, 20 Shutterstock.com.

Printed in the United States of America

CPSIA compliance information: Batch #CW11GS: For further information contact Gareth Stevens, New York, New York at 1-800-542-2595.

Contents

Words in the glossary appear in **bold** type the first time they are used in the text.

What Is a Pulling Dog?

A pulling dog, or draft dog, moves carts or sleds. This dog-powered movement is called mushing. The dogs are connected to the cart or sled by a **harness**. These dogs are strong and must be well trained. Sometimes, pulling dogs are trained to **compete** against other dogs.

There are two types of pulling dogs—sled dogs and cart dogs. Both move people and **cargo**.

4

These dogs are competing in a sled race.

Dog Tales

Huskies have two layers of fur to keep them warm in very cold temperatures.

Sled dogs like these Siberian huskies are used to running in the snow. ▷

Sled Dogs

Sled dogs work in very cold places. They pull sleds over snow and ice. The best sled dogs weigh 55 pounds (25 kg) or less, but they can pull hundreds of pounds!

Many types of dogs can pull sleds. The most common sled dogs are called "huskies." Huskies are loving and smart. They are good at following orders if they have firm leaders. There are many different kinds of huskies.

7

Popular Sled Dogs

Siberian huskies usually have white fur with some red, gray, or black. They have blue, brown, or yellowish eyes. They are very friendly dogs.

The Alaskan malamute usually has white fur and some red, gray, or black fur, too. Malamutes are bigger than Siberian huskies and can pull a lot of weight a long way.

The Samoyed is all white. It comes from a long line of working dogs raised by the Samoyed people of Siberia.

Dog Tales

Huskies have tender feet. Sometimes, they wear booties to **protect** their feet when they pull sleds.

The different types of huskies look very much alike. It can be hard to tell a Siberian husky from an Alaskan malamute.

Dog Tales

Dogsled racing became a sport in 1908 with the All-Alaska Sweepstakes race.

These sled dogs must work as a team and follow directions from the sled driver.

10

Sled Dog Racing

Today, many sled dogs compete in races. They may pull alone or in a team. A team can have as many as 200 dogs! Each dog has a role. The lead dog takes directions from the sled driver. Point or swing dogs help the lead dog. Wheel dogs are the closest to the sled. They are larger dogs able to keep heavy sleds on the trail. The other dogs, called team dogs, provide extra power and **endurance** for their team.

The Iditarod

The Iditarod is held in Alaska and is the most famous dogsled race. It is about 1,150 miles (1,850 km) long and takes 10 to 17 days to finish! Dog teams race between Anchorage and Nome.

The race honors the Great Race of Mercy. During an **epidemic** in 1925, a dogsled team carried **medicine** to Nome in a bad snowstorm. In the late 1800s and early 1900s, some of the Iditarod trail was traveled by dogsleds carrying mail, supplies, and gold, too.

Dog Tales

Sled dogs eat almost 10 times their usual diet when racing in the Iditarod.

Bigger sleds are used in longer races. Sled drivers bring food and water for themselves and the dogs.

13

It is important to let pulling dogs rest when they are on the trail.

14

Cart Dogs

Throughout history, cart dogs have helped people with transportation. They might even carry a load tied to their backs. Any dog can be trained in carting, as long as it obeys its **handler**. Large dogs are the most common cart dogs.

Carting has become a popular hobby for some dog owners. It is good exercise for the dog. Dogs of many **breeds** compete in pulling different weights and distances. Some competitions ask dogs to **maneuver** carts around objects.

Popular Cart Dogs

The Bernese mountain dog has a black body, white chest, and rust-colored fur above its eyes. The Bernese is gentle, good natured, and can weigh up to 110 pounds (50 kg).

Newfoundlands are sweet dogs who love water. They are black, gray, or brown. A male Newfoundland can weigh as much as 150 pounds (68 kg)!

Greater Swiss mountain dogs have worked on farms in the mountains for many years. They are brave dogs and weigh about 130 pounds (59 kg) when grown.

Dog Tales

In their homeland of Newfoundland, Canada, Newfoundland dogs helped fishermen pull in fishing nets.

Dogs like this Newfoundland don't have to compete to enjoy carting.

17

Puppies start to wear a harness early so they are comfortable with it as adults.

Training

Many draft dogs start training as puppies. The puppies may start wearing the harness used for pulling when they are as young as 6 months old. They train to gain strength, speed, and endurance by pulling long distances and short distances with many different amounts of weight.

Pulling dogs have a special **relationship** with their handlers. Handlers must establish themselves as the alpha, or leader, of their dogs, especially during training.

Talking to a Pulling Dog

Handlers use voice commands to control their dogs. These words are very important in competitions when a handler must tell a dog what to do. The most important commands include words for "slow down," "stop," and "go."

Commands for Pulling Dogs

Voice Command	Meaning
hike/giddy up/walk on	start to pull
whoa/stop	stop pulling
easy	slow down
gee	turn right
haw	turn left
on by	go straight or pass

21

Glossary

breed: a group of animals that share features different from other groups of that kind

cargo: goods carried by a cart

compete: to try to win in a game

endurance: the ability to do something hard for a long time

epidemic: a rapidly spreading illness

handler: a person who trains and controls an animal

harness: straps around an animal that allow a driver to control it

maneuver: to move around skillfully

medicine: something used to treat sickness

protect: to keep safe

relationship: a connection between people, animals, or things

For More Information

Books:

Cary, Bob. *Born to Pull: The Glory of Sled Dogs.* Minneapolis, MN: University of Minnesota Press, 2009.

Haskins, Lori. *Sled Dogs.* New York, NY: Bearport Publishing, 2006.

Web Sites:

Dog Carting
http://doghobbyist.com/articles/DogHobbyist/Carting.html
Read how you can teach your dog to pull a cart.

The Official Site of the Iditarod
www.iditarod.com
Find out more about the Iditarod.

Index